INSIGHTS
The Lord's Prayer

INSIGHTS

The Lord's Prayer

What the Bible Tells Us about The Lord's Prayer

WILLIAM BARCLAY

SAINT ANDREW PRESS
Edinburgh

First published in 2008 by
SAINT ANDREW PRESS
121 George Street
Edinburgh EH2 4YN

ISBN 978 0 7152 0859 5

British Library Cataloguing in Publication Data
A catalogue record for this book is available from the British Library

It is the Publisher's policy to only use papers that are natural and
recyclable and that have been manufactured from timber grown in
renewable, properly managed forests. All of the manufacturing
processes of the papers are expected to conform to the environmental
regulations of the country of origin.

Typeset by Waverley Typesetters, Fakenham
Printed and bound by Bell & Bain Ltd, Glasgow

Contents

Foreword by
The Right Revd Richard Harries

(Lord Harries of Pentregarth, the former Bishop of Oxford, Gresham Professor of Divinity and Honorary Professor of Theology at King's College, London)

There are a number of reasons why I am glad to write this introduction. My father always found William Barclay's commentaries helpful, and those small red-covered volumes were a familiar sight on his shelves. He had not always been a churchgoer. Indeed my mother said that for many years she could not get him inside a church even for Christmas. But later in life he came back to faith in a serious way and was much nourished by the Christian mystics on the one hand, and William Barclay on the other.

In 1958 I went off to Cambridge to read theology and was inducted into historical and critical approaches to the Bible, but I later joined my father in an appreciation of Barclay. For he was, of course, a distinguished scholar and in his commentaries you could always find much useful background material made readily accessible. But, unlike too much academic writing, he expressed himself with extraordinary clarity. This, together with his penchant for a telling quotation and good story, made him highly readable.

Although a distinguished professional scholar, he never ceased to write primarily as a follower to Jesus to fellow disciples. Most scholarship is just that. Most devotional writing sits too light to the historical and critical facts. Barclay was one of the few who could at the same time distill the essence of scholarly findings with nourishment for the Christian way. Moreover his approach, though seasoned by Scottish history and culture, like that of C.S.Lewis, was for Christians of all persuasions. Like him he would have been happy to call it 'Mere Christianity'.

I am particularly glad to be writing an introduction to what William Barclay wrote on the Lord's Prayer. Perhaps, not surprisingly, this is a prayer that never palls, never stales. Time and again it can lift us out of self-preoccupation into the Divine Purpose for the world. If it is not too banal I think of the Lord's Prayer like a decently boiled egg, which one could eat everyday of one's life without its losing its savour. Day by day it nourishes. If a person prayed nothing but the Lord's Prayer they could not go wrong. Hardly surprising, in fact, for Jesus gave us this as the model and form of all prayer. There are a few phrases in the prayer that are puzzling and this is where sound scholarship can come to our aid, helping us to enter into the mind of Jesus for the world.

This is, as Barclay emphasises, above all a prayer for adults; for adults who wish to walk the Christian way. I believe a new generation of Christians will find William Barclay's *Insights* on the Lord's Prayer as helpful as millions of others before them have done.

RICHARD HARRIES
King's College, London

Publisher's Introduction

'Give us this day our daily bread'.

There are many meanings of this familiar and deceptively simple request. At its simplest, it is a request for the *provisions* we need for each day. But it can also be linked to the *communion* table, where Jesus asked us to break bread in memory of him. And it may also refer to *spiritual* food, making it an appeal for the essential truth of life. And it may also refer to *Jesus*, who called himself the bread of life. So the Lord's Prayer is a prayer that daily we may be strenghtened by him who is the living bread.

In the *Insights* series, William Barclay takes the original Greek of the Scriptures, translates it into modern language, and explains it in a way we can all understand. We learn some surprising things. For example, we learn how prayer really works: the Lord's Prayer does not mean that we just pray and then wait for bread to fall into our hands. It is a subtle reminder that when we pray for bread we must go on to plant the seed. Prayer and work go hand in hand.

Insights: The Lord's Prayer also shows how the Lord's Prayer fits in with the Gospels according Matthew and Luke. Each writer was writing at a particular time and for a particular reason. *Insights* makes no assumptions about our knowledge, but enables us to understand the Bible in new ways by starting with something familiar and then finding some surprising twists in the tale.

The Gospel of Matthew –
setting the context

The gospel of the Jews

First and foremost, Matthew *is the gospel which was written for the Jews*. It was written by a Jew in order to convince Jews.One of the great objects of Matthew is to demonstrate that all the prophecies of the Old Testament are fulfilled in Jesus, and that, therefore, he must be the Messiah. It has one phrase which runs through it like an ever-recurring theme: 'This was to fulfil what the Lord had spoken by the prophet.' That phrase occurs in the gospel as often as sixteen times. Jesus' birth and Jesus' name are the fulfilment of prophecy (1:21–3); so are the flight to Egypt (2:14–15); the slaughter of the children (2:16–18); Joseph's settlement in Nazareth and Jesus' upbringing there (2:23); Jesus' use of parables (3:34–5); the triumphal entry (21:3–5); the betrayal for thirty pieces of silver (27:9); and the casting of lots for Jesus' garments as he hung on the cross (27:35). It is Matthew's primary and deliberate purpose to show how the Old Testament prophecies received their fulfilment in Jesus; how every detail of Jesus' life was foreshadowed in the prophets; and thus to compel the Jews to admit that Jesus was the Messiah.

The main interest of Matthew is in the Jews. Their conversion is especially near and dear to the heart of its writer.

When the Syro-Phoenician woman seeks his help, Jesus' first answer is: 'I was sent only to the lost sheep of the house of Israel' (15:24). When Jesus sends out the Twelve on the task of evangelization, his instruction is: 'Go nowhere among the Gentiles, and enter no town of the Samaritans, but go rather to the lost sheep of the house of Israel' (10:5–6). Yet it is not to be thought that this gospel by any means excludes the Gentiles. Many are to come from the east and the west to sit down in the kingdom of God (8:11). The gospel is to be preached to the whole world (24:14). And it is Matthew which gives us the marching orders of the Church: 'Go therefore and make disciples of all nations' (28:19). It is clear that Matthew's first interest is in the Jews, but that it foresees the day when all nations will be gathered in.

The teaching gospel

The apostle Matthew was responsible for the first collection and the first handbook of the teaching of Jesus. Matthew was the great systematizer. It was his habit to gather together in one place all that he knew about the teaching of Jesus on any given subject. The result is that in Matthew we find five great blocks in which the teaching of Jesus is collected and systematized. All these sections have to do with the kingdom of God. They are as follows:

(a) The Sermon on the Mount, or the law of the kingdom (5–7).
(b) The duties of the leaders of the kingdom (10).
(c) The parables of the kingdom (13).
(d) Greatness and forgiveness in the kingdom (18).
(e) The coming of the King (24–5).

Matthew does more than collect and systematize. It must be remembered that Matthew was writing in an age when printing had not been invented, when books were few and far between because they had to be handwritten. In an age like that, comparatively few people could possess a book; and, therefore, if they wished to know and to use the teaching and the story of Jesus, they had to carry them in their memories.

Matthew therefore always arranges things in a way that is easy for the reader to memorize. He arranges things in threes and sevens. There are three messages to Joseph; three denials of Peter; three questions of Pilate; seven parables of the kingdom in chapter 13; and seven woes to the scribes and Pharisees in chapter 23.

Matthew has one final characteristic. Matthew's *dominating idea is that of Jesus as King*. He writes to demonstrate the royalty of Jesus.

Right at the beginning, the genealogy is to prove that Jesus is the Son of David (1:1–17). The title, Son of David, is used more often in Matthew than in any other gospel (15:22, 21:9, 21:15). The wise men come looking for him who is King of the Jews (2:2). The triumphal entry is a deliberately dramatized claim to be King (21:1–11). Before Pilate, Jesus deliberately accepts the name of King (27:11). Even on the cross, the title of King is affixed, even if it is in mockery, over his head (27:37). In the Sermon on the Mount, Matthew shows us Jesus quoting the law and five times abrogating it with a regal: 'But I say to you …' (5:22, 28, 34, 39, 44). The final claim of Jesus is: 'All authority … has been given to me' (28:18).

The Lord's Prayer according to the Gospel of Matthew

How not to pray

Matthew 6:5–8

> 'And when you pray, you must not be like the hypocrites,
> for they are fond of praying standing in the synagogues and
> at the corners of the streets, so that they may be seen by
> people. This is the truth I tell you – they are paid in full. But
> when you pray, go into your private room, and shut the door,
> and pray to your Father who is in secret; and your Father
> who sees what happens in secret will give you your reward
> in full.
>
> 'When you pray, do not pile up meaningless phrases, as
> the Gentiles do, for their idea is that they will be heard
> because of the length of their words. So, then, do not be like
> them, for your Father knows the things you need before you
> ask him.'

No nation ever had a higher ideal of prayer than the Jews
had; and no religion ever ranked prayer higher in the scale of
priorities than the Jews did. 'Great is prayer,' said the Rabbis,
'greater than all good works.' One of the loveliest things that
was ever said about family worship is the Rabbinic saying:
'He who prays within his house surrounds it with a wall that

is stronger than iron.' The only regret of the Rabbis was that it was not possible to pray all day long.

But certain faults had crept into the habits of prayer. It is to be noted that these faults are by no means peculiar to Jewish ideas of prayer; they can and do occur anywhere. And it is to be noted that they could only occur in a community where prayer was taken with the greatest seriousness. They are not the faults of neglect; they are the faults of misguided devotion.

(1) Prayer tended to become formalized. There were two things the daily use of which was prescribed for every Jew.

The first was the *Shema*, which consists of three short passages of Scripture – Deuteronomy 6:4–9, 11:13–21; Numbers 15:37–41. *Shema* is the imperative of the Hebrew word for *to hear*, and the *Shema* takes its name from the verse which was the essence and centre of the whole matter: 'Hear, O Israel, the Lord our God is one Lord.'

The full *Shema* had to be recited by every Jew every morning and every evening. It had to be said as early as possible. It had to be said as soon as the light was strong enough to distinguish between blue and white, or, as Rabbi Eliezer said, between blue and green. In any event, it had to be said before the third hour, that is, 9 am; and in the evening it had to be said before 9 pm. If the last possible moment for the saying of the *Shema* had come, no matter where a man found himself, at home, in the street, at work or in the synagogue, he must stop and say it.

There were many who loved the *Shema*, and who repeated it with reverence and adoration and love; but inevitably there were still more who gabbled their way through it and went their way. The *Shema* had every chance of becoming a vain repetition, which was mumbled like some incantation. Christians are but ill-qualified to criticize, for everything that has been said about formally gabbling through the *Shema* can be said about grace before meals in many families

The second thing which every Jew had to repeat daily was called the *Shemonēh 'esreh*, which means *the Eighteen*. It consisted of eighteen prayers, and was, and still is, an essential part of the synagogue service. In time the prayers became nineteen, but the old name remains. Most of these prayers are quite short, and nearly all of them are very lovely.

The twelfth runs:

Let Thy mercy, O Lord, be showed upon the upright, the humble, the elders of thy people Israel, and the rest of its teachers; be favourable to the pious strangers among us, and to us all. Give thou a good reward to those who sincerely trust in thy name, that our lot may be cast among them in the world to come, that our hope be not deceived. Praised be thou, O Lord, who art the hope and confidence of the faithful.

The fifth runs:

Bring us back to thy law, O our Father; bring us back, O King, to thy service; bring us back to thee by true repentance. Praised be thou, O Lord, who dost accept our repentance.

No church possesses a more beautiful liturgy than the *Shemonēh 'esreh*. The law was that Jews must recite it three times a day – once in the morning, once in the afternoon and once in the evening. The same thing happened again. Devout Jews prayed it with loving devotion; but there were many to whom this series of lovely prayers became a gabbled formula. There was even a summary supplied which might be prayed, if there was not the time to repeat the whole eighteen or they could not all be remembered. The repetition of the *Shemonēh 'esreh* became nothing more than a superstitious incantation. Again, Christians are ill-qualified to criticize, for there are many occasions when they do precisely the same with the prayer which Christ taught them to pray.

How not to pray

Matthew 6:5–8 (*contd*)

(2) FURTHER, the Jewish liturgy supplied stated prayers for all occasions. There was hardly an event or a sight in life which had not its stated formula of prayer. There was prayer before and after each meal; there were prayers in connection with the light, the fire and the lightning, on seeing the new moon, on comets, rain or tempest, at the sight of the sea, lakes or rivers, on receiving good news, on using new furniture, on entering or leaving a city. Everything had its prayer. Clearly, there is something infinitely lovely here. It was the intention that every happening in life should be brought into the presence of God.

But just because the prayers were so meticulously prescribed and stated, the whole system lent itself to formalism, and the danger was for the prayers to slip off the tongue with very little meaning. The tendency was glibly to repeat the right prayer at the right time. The great Rabbis knew that and tried to guard against it. 'If a man', they said, 'says his prayers, as if to get through a set task, that is no prayer.' 'Do not look on prayer as a formal duty, but as an act of humility by which to obtain the mercy of God.' Rabbi Eliezer was so impressed with the danger of formalism that it was his custom to compose one new prayer every day, that his prayer might be always fresh. It is quite clear that this kind of danger is not confined to Jewish religion. Even quiet times which began in devotion can end in the formalism of a rigid and ritualistic timetable.

(3) Still further, devout Jews prayed at regular times, always in the morning and the evening, and sometimes also at noon. Wherever they found themselves, they were bound to pray. Clearly, they might be genuinely remembering God, or they might be carrying out a habitual formality.

Muslims have the same custom. It is a lovely thing that three times a day people should remember God; but there is a real danger that it may come to no more than this – that three times a day the prayers are spoken without a thought of God.

(4) There was a tendency to connect prayer with certain places, and especially with the synagogue. It is undeniably true that there are certain places where God seems very near; but there were certain Rabbis who went to the lengths of saying that prayer was efficacious only if it was offered in the Temple or in the synagogue. So there grew up the custom of going to the Temple at the hours of prayer. In the first days of the Christian Church, even the disciples of Jesus thought in terms like these, for we read of Peter and John going up to the Temple at the hour of prayer (Acts 3:1).

There was a danger here, the danger that people might come to think of God as being confined to certain holy places and that they might forget that the whole earth is the temple of God. The wisest of the Rabbis saw this danger. They said: 'God says to Israel, pray in the synagogue of your city; if you cannot, pray in the field; if you cannot, pray in your house; if you cannot, pray on your bed; if you cannot, commune with your own heart upon your bed, and be still.'

The trouble about any system lies not in the system, but in those who use it. It is possible to make any system of prayer an instrument of devotion or a formality, glibly and unthinkingly to be gone through.

(5) There was among the Jews an undoubted tendency towards long prayers. That was a tendency by no means confined to the Jews. In eighteenth-century worship in Scotland, length meant devotion. In such a Scottish service, there was a verse-by-verse lecture on Scripture which lasted for an hour, and a sermon which lasted for another hour. Prayers were lengthy and spontaneous. The liturgist Dr W. D. Maxwell writes: 'The efficacy of prayer was measured by its ardour and its fluency, and not least by its fervid lengthiness.' Rabbi Levi said: 'Whoever is long in prayer is heard.' Another saying has it: 'Whenever the righteous make their prayer long, their prayer is heard.'

There was – and still is – a kind of subconscious idea that if we batter long enough at God's door, he will answer; that God can be talked, and even pestered, into condescension. The wisest Rabbis were well aware of this danger. One of them said: 'It is forbidden to lengthen out the praise of the Holy One. It says in the Psalms: "*Who can* utter the mighty doings of the Lord, or show forth all his praise?" [Psalm

106:2]. There only *he who can* may lengthen out and tell his praise – *but no one can.*' 'Let a man's words before God always be few, as it is said, "Be not rash with your mouth, and let not your heart be hasty to utter a word before God; for God is in heaven, and you upon earth, therefore let your words be few" [Ecclesiastes 5:2].' 'The best adoration consists in keeping silence.' It is easy to confound verbosity with piety, and fluency with devotion – and into that mistake many people fell.

How not to pray

Matthew 6:5–8 (*contd*)

(6) THERE were certain other forms of repetition, which the Jews, like all people of the middle east, were apt to use and to overuse. People had a habit of hypnotizing themselves by the endless repetition of one phrase or even of one word. In 1 Kings 18:26, we read how the prophets of Baal cried out: 'O Baal answer us', for the space of half a day. In Acts 19:34, we read how the Ephesian mob, for two hours, kept shouting: 'Great is Artemis of the Ephesians.' Muslims will go on repeating the sacred syllable *He* for hours on end. The Jews did that with the *Shema*. It is a kind of substitution of self-hypnotism for prayer.

There was another way in which Jewish prayer used repetition. There was an attempt to pile up every possible title and adjective in the address of the prayer to God. One famous prayer begins:

Blessed, praised, and glorified, exalted, extolled and honoured, magnified and lauded be the name of the Holy One.

There is one Jewish prayer which actually begins with sixteen different adjectives attached to the name of God. There was a kind of intoxication with words. When people begin to think more of how they are praying than of what they are praying, their prayers die upon their lips.

(7) The final fault which Jesus found with certain of the Jews was that they prayed in order to be seen. The Jewish system of prayer made ostentation very easy. Jews prayed standing, with hands stretched out, palms upwards, and with heads bowed. Prayer had to be said in the morning and in the evening. It had to be said wherever they might be, and it was easy for people to make sure that at these hours they were at a busy street corner, or in a crowded city square, so that all the world might see with what devotion they prayed. It was easy to halt on the top step of the entrance to the synagogue, and there pray lengthily and demonstratively, so that all might admire such exceptional piety. It was easy to put on an act of prayer which all the world might see.

The wisest of the Jewish Rabbis fully understood and unsparingly condemned this attitude. 'A man in whom is hypocrisy brings wrath upon the world, and his prayer is not heard.' 'Four classes of men do not receive the face of the glory of God – the mockers, the hypocrites, the liars and the slanderers.' The Rabbis said that no man could pray at all unless his heart was attuned to pray. They laid it down that for perfect prayer there were necessary an hour of private preparation beforehand and an hour of meditation afterwards. But the Jewish system of prayer did lend itself to ostentation, if in a person's heart there was pride.

In effect, Jesus lays down two great rules for prayer.

(1) He insists that all true prayer must be offered to God. The real fault of the people whom Jesus was criticizing was that they were praying to others and not to God. A certain great preacher once described an ornate and elaborate prayer offered in a Boston church as 'the most eloquent prayer ever offered to a Boston audience'. The preacher was much more concerned with impressing the congregation than with making contact with God. Whether in public or in private prayer, we should have no thought in our minds and no desire in our hearts but God.

(2) He insists that we must always remember that the God to whom we pray is a God of love who is more ready to answer than we are to pray. His gifts and his grace have not to be unwillingly extracted from him. We do not come to a God who has to be coaxed, or pestered, or battered into answering our prayers. We come to one whose one wish is to give. When we remember that, it is surely sufficient to go to God with the sigh of desire in our hearts, and on our lips the words 'Your will be done.'

The disciple's prayer

Matthew 6:9–15

> *'So, then, pray in this way:*
> *Our Father in heaven, let your name be held holy:*

Let your kingdom come:
Let your will be done, as in heaven, so also on earth:
Give us today bread for the coming day:
Forgive us our debts as we forgive our debtors:
And lead us not into temptation, but deliver us from
        the evil one.
For, if you forgive men their trespasses, your heavenly
        Father will forgive you too; but if you do not forgive men
        their trespasses, neither will your Father forgive your
        trespasses.'

BEFORE we begin to think about the Lord's Prayer in detail, there are certain general facts which we will do well to remember about it.

We must note, first of all, that this is a prayer which Jesus taught his *disciples* to pray. Both Matthew and Luke are clear about that. Matthew sets the whole Sermon on the Mount in the context of the disciples (Matthew 5:1); and Luke tells us that Jesus taught this prayer in response to the request of one of his disciples (Luke 11:1). The Lord's Prayer is a prayer which only a disciple can pray; it is a prayer which only those who are committed to Jesus Christ can take upon their lips with any meaning.

The Lord's Prayer is not a child's prayer, as it is so often regarded; it is, in fact, not meaningful for a child. The Lord's Prayer is not the Family Prayer as it is sometimes called, unless by the word *family* we mean *the family of the Church*. The Lord's Prayer is specifically and definitely stated to be the *disciple's* prayer; and only on the lips of a disciple has the prayer its full meaning. To put it in another way, the Lord's Prayer can only really be prayed when those who pray it know what they are saying, and they cannot know that until they have entered into discipleship.

We must note the *order* of the petitions in the Lord's Prayer. The first three petitions have to do with God and with the glory of God; the second three petitions have to do with our needs and our necessities. That is to say, God is first given his supreme place – and then, and only then, do we turn to ourselves and our needs and desires. It is only when God is given his proper place that all other things fall into their proper places. Prayer must never be an attempt to bend the will of God to our desires; prayer ought always to be an attempt to submit our wills to the will of God.

The second part of the prayer, the part which deals with our needs and our necessities, is a marvellously created unity. It deals with the three essential human needs and the three spheres of time within which we all move. First, it asks for *bread*, for that which is necessary for the *maintenance of life*, and thereby brings the needs of the *present* to the throne of God. Second, it asks for *forgiveness* and thereby brings the *past* into the presence of God. Third, it asks for *help in temptation* and thereby commits all the future into the hands of God. In these three brief petitions, we are taught to lay the present, the past and the future before the footstool of the grace of God.

But not only is this a prayer which brings the whole of life to the presence of God; it is also a prayer which brings the whole of God to our lives. When we ask for *bread* to sustain our earthly lives, that request immediately directs our thoughts to *God the Father*, the Creator and the Sustainer of all life. When we ask for *forgiveness*, that request immediately directs our thoughts to *God the Son*, Jesus Christ our Saviour and Redeemer. When we ask for help for future temptation, that request immediately directs our thoughts to *God the Holy Spirit*, the Comforter, the Strengthener, the Illuminator, the Guide and the Guardian of our way.

In the most amazing way, this brief second part of the Lord's Prayer takes the present, the past and the future, the whole of human life, and presents them to God the Father, God the Son and God the Holy Spirit, to God in all his fullness. In the Lord's Prayer, Jesus teaches us to bring the whole of life to the whole of God, and to bring the whole of God to the whole of life.

The Father in heaven

Matthew 6:9

> *Our Father in heaven.*

It might well be said that the word *Father* used of God is a compact summary of the Christian faith. The great value of this word *Father* is that it settles all the relationships of this life.

(1) *It settles our relationship to the unseen world.* Missionaries tell us that one of the greatest reliefs which Christianity brings to the minds and hearts of those who hold a primitive religious belief is the certainty that there is only one God. For those who hold such beliefs, there are hordes of gods; every stream and river, and tree and valley, and hill and wood, and every natural force has its own god. Their world is crowded with gods. Still further, all these gods are jealous, grudging and hostile. They must all be placated, and people can never be sure that they have not omitted the honour due to some of these gods. The

consequence is that the people live in terror of the gods; they are haunted and not helped by their religion.

The most significant Greek legend of the gods is the legend of Prometheus. Prometheus was a god. It was in the days before people possessed fire; and life without fire was a cheerless and a comfortless thing. In pity, Prometheus took fire from heaven and gave it as a gift to human beings. Zeus, the king of the gods, was mightily angry that they should receive this gift. So he took Prometheus and chained him to a rock in the middle of the Adriatic Sea, where he was tortured with the heat and the thirst of the day and with the cold of the night. Even more, Zeus prepared a vulture to tear out Prometheus' liver, which always grew again, only to be torn out again.

That is what happened to the god who tried to help men and women. The whole conception is that the gods are jealous, vengeful and grudging; and the last thing the gods wish to do is to help the human race. That is the pagan idea of the attitude of the unseen world to human beings, and it means that people are haunted by the fear of a horde of jealous and grudging gods. So, when we discover that the God to whom we pray has the name and the heart of a *father*, it makes literally all the difference in the world. We need no longer shiver before a horde of jealous gods; we can rest in a father's love.

(2) *It settles our relationship to the seen world*, to this world of space and time in which we live. It is easy to think of this world as a hostile world. There are the chances and the changes of life; there are the iron laws of the universe which we break at our peril; there is suffering and death; but if we can be sure that behind this world there is not a capricious, jealous, mocking god, but a God whose name is

Father, then although much may still remain dark, all is now bearable because behind all is love. It will always help us if we regard this world as organized not for our comfort but for our training.

Take, for instance, *pain*. Pain might seem a bad thing, but pain has its place in the order of God. It sometimes happens that people are constituted in such a way that they are incapable of feeling pain. Such people are a danger to themselves and a problem to everyone else. If there were no such thing as pain, we would never know that we were ill, and often we would die before steps could be taken to deal with any disease or illness. That is not to say that pain cannot *become* a bad thing, but it is to say that more often than not pain is God's red light to tell us that there is danger ahead.

The eighteenth-century German scholar G. E. Lessing used to say that if he had one question to ask the Sphinx, it would be: 'Is this a friendly universe?' If we can be certain that the name of the God who created this world is *Father*, then we can also be certain that fundamentally this is a friendly universe. To call God *Father* is to settle our relationship to the world in which we live.

The Father in heaven

Matthew 6:9 (*contd*)

(3) IF we believe that God is Father, *it settles our relationship to one another*. If God is Father, he is Father of all people. The Lord's Prayer does not teach us to pray *My Father*; it teaches us to pray *Our Father*. It is very significant that in the Lord's

Prayer the words *I*, *me* and *mine* never occur; it is true to say that Jesus came to take these words out of life and to put in their place *we*, *us* and *ours*. God is no one's exclusive possession. The very phrase *Our Father* involves *the elimination of self*. The fatherhood of God is the only possible basis of human relationships.

(4) If we believe that God is Father, *it settles our relationship to ourselves*. There are times for each and every one of us when we despise and hate ourselves. We know that we are lower than the lowest thing that crawls upon the earth. The heart knows its own bitterness, and no one knows our unworthiness better than we do ourselves.

The writer Mark Rutherford wished to add a new beatitude: 'Blessed are those who heal us of our self-despisings.' Blessed are those who give us back our self-respect. That is precisely what God does. In these grim, bleak, terrible moments, we can still remind ourselves that, even if we matter to no one else, we matter to God; that in the infinite mercy of God we are of royal lineage, children of the King of Kings.

(5) If we believe that God is Father, *it settles our relationship to God*. It is not that it removes the might, majesty and power of God. It is not that it makes God any the less God; but it makes that might, and majesty, and power approachable for us.

There is an old Roman story which tells how a Roman emperor was enjoying a triumph. He had the privilege, which Rome gave to her great victors, of marching his troops through the streets of Rome, with all his captured trophies and his prisoners in his train. So the emperor was on the march with his troops. The streets were lined with cheering people. The tall legionaries lined the streets' edges to keep the people in their places. At one point on the triumphal route, there was a little platform where the empress and her family were sitting to watch the emperor go by in all the pride of his triumph. On the platform with his mother, there was the emperor's youngest son, a little boy. As the emperor came near, the little boy jumped off the platform, burrowed through the crowd and tried to dodge between the legs of a legionary and to run out on to the road to meet his father's chariot. The legionary stooped down and stopped him. He swung him up in his arms: 'You can't do that, boy,' he said. 'Don't you know who that is in the chariot? That's the emperor. You can't run out to his chariot.' And the little boy laughed down. 'He may be your emperor,' he said, 'but he's my father.' That is exactly the way the Christian feels towards God. The might, and the majesty, and the power are the might, and the majesty, and the power of one whom Jesus taught us to call *Our Father*.

The Father in heaven

Matthew 6:9 (*contd*)

So far, we have been thinking of the first two words of this address to God – *Our Father*; but God is not only *Our Father*, he is Our Father *who is in heaven*. The last words are of primary importance. They conserve two great truths.

(1) They remind us of the *holiness* of God. It is very easy to cheapen and to sentimentalize the whole idea of the fatherhood of God, and to make it an excuse for an easygoing, comfortable religion. 'He's a good fellow and all will be well.' As the German poet Heinrich Heine said of God: 'God will

forgive. It is his trade.' If we were to say *Our Father*, and stop there, there might be some excuse for that; but it is Our Father *in heaven* to whom we pray. The love is there, but the holiness is there, too.

It is extraordinary how seldom Jesus used the word Father in regard to God. Mark's gospel is the earliest gospel, and is therefore the nearest thing we will ever have to an actual report of all that Jesus said and did; and in Mark's gospel Jesus calls God *Father* only six times, and never outside the circle of the disciples. To Jesus, the word *Father* was so sacred that he could hardly bear to use it; and he could never use it except among those who had grasped something of what it meant.

We must never use the word *Father* in regard to God cheaply, easily and sentimentally. God is not an easy-going parent who tolerantly shuts his eyes to all sins and faults and mistakes. This God, whom we can call Father, is the God whom we must still approach with reverence and adoration, and awe and wonder. God is our Father in heaven, and in God there is *love* and *holiness* combined.

(2) They remind us of the *power* of God. In human love, there is so often the tragedy of frustration. We may love people and yet be unable to help them achieve something, or to stop them doing something. Human love can be intense – and quite helpless. Any parent with an erring child, or any lover with a wandering loved one, knows that. But when we say *Our Father – in heaven*, we place two things side by side. We place side by side the *love* of God and the *power* of God. We tell ourselves that the power of God is always motivated by the love of God, and can never be exercised for anything but our good; we tell ourselves that the love of God is backed by the power of God, and that therefore its

purposes can never be ultimately frustrated or defeated. It is love of which we think, but it is the love of God. When we pray *Our Father in heaven*, we must always remember the holiness of God, and we must always remember the power which moves in love, and the love which has behind it the undefeatable power of God.

The hallowing of the name

Matthew 6:9 (*contd*)

> *Let your name be held holy.*

'HALLOWED be your name' – it is probably true that of all the petitions of the Lord's Prayer this is the one whose meaning we would find it most difficult to express. First, then, let us concentrate on the actual meaning of the words.

The word which is translated as *hallowed* is a part of the Greek verb *hagiazesthai*. The Greek verb *hagiazesthai* is connected with the adjective *hagios*, and means *to treat a person or a thing as hagios*. *Hagios* is the word which is usually translated as *holy*; but the basic meaning of *hagios* is *different* or *separate*. A thing which is *hagios* is *different* from other things. A person who is *hagios* is *separate* from other people. So, a temple is *hagios* because it is *different* from other buildings. An altar is *hagios* because it exists for a purpose *different* from the purpose of ordinary things. God's day is *hagios* because it is *different* from other days. Priests are *hagios* because they are *separate* from other people. So, this petition means: 'Let God's name be treated differently from all other names; let God's name be given a position which is absolutely unique.'

But there is something to add to this. In Hebrew, the *name* does not mean simply the name by which a person is called – John or James, or whatever the name may be. In Hebrew, the *name* means the *nature*, the *character*, the *personality* of the person in so far as it is known or revealed to us. That becomes clear when we see how the Bible writers use the expression.

The psalmist says: 'Those who know your *name* put their trust in you' (Psalm 9:10). Quite clearly, that does not mean that those who know that God is called Yahweh will trust in him. It means that those who know what God is like, those who know the nature and the character of God, will put their trust in him. The psalmist says: 'Some take pride in chariots, and some in horses, but our pride is in the *name* of the Lord our God' (Psalm 20:7). Quite clearly, that does not mean that in a time of difficulty the psalmist will remember that God is called Yahweh. It means that at such a time some will put their trust in human and material aids and defences, but the psalmist will remember the nature and the character of God; he will remember what God is like, and that memory will give him confidence.

So, let us take these two things and put them together. *Hagiazesthai*, which is translated as *to hallow*, means *to regard as different*, to give a unique and special place to. The *name* is the *nature*, the *character*, the *personality* of the person in so far as it is known and revealed to us. Therefore, when we pray 'Hallowed be your name,' it means: 'Enable us to give to you the unique place which your nature and character deserve and demand.'

The prayer for reverence

Matthew 6:9 (*contd*)

Is there, then, one word in English for giving to God the unique place which his nature and character demand? There is such a word, and the word is *reverence*. This petition is a prayer that we should be enabled to show reverence for God as God deserves to be reverenced. In all true reverence of God, there are four essentials.

(1) In order to show reverence for God, we must believe that God exists. We cannot show reverence for someone who does not exist; we must begin by being sure of the existence of God.

To the modern mind, it is strange that the Bible nowhere attempts to prove the existence of God. For the Bible, God is an axiom. An axiom is a self-evident fact which is not itself proved, but which is the basis of all other proofs. For instance, 'A straight line is the shortest distance between two points' and 'Parallel lines, however far produced, will never meet' are axioms.

The Bible writers would have said that it was superfluous to prove the existence of God, because they *experienced* the presence of God every moment of their lives. They would have said that there was no more need to prove that God exists than the need for a husband to prove that his wife exists, or a wife her husband. The husband and wife meet every day, and they meet God every day.

But suppose we did need to try to prove that God exists, using our own minds to do so, how would we begin? We might begin from *the world in which we live*. William Paley's old argument, produced at the beginning of the nineteenth century, is not yet completely outdated. Suppose there is a man walking along the road. He strikes his foot against a watch lying in the dust. He has never in his life seen a watch before; he does not know what it is. He picks it up; he sees that it consists of a metal case, and inside the case a complicated arrangement of wheels, levers, springs and jewels. He sees that the whole thing is moving and working in the most orderly way. He sees further that the hands are moving round the dial in an obviously predetermined routine. What then does he say? Does he say: 'All these metals and jewels came together from the ends of the earth by chance, by chance made themselves into wheels and levers and springs, by chance assembled themselves into this mechanism, by chance wound themselves up and set themselves going, by chance acquired their obvious orderly working'? No. He says: 'I have found a watch; somewhere there must be a watchmaker.'

Order presupposes mind. We look at the world; we see a vast machine which is working in order. Suns rise and set in an unvarying succession. Tides ebb and flow to a timetable. Seasons follow each other in an order. We look at the world, and we are bound to say: 'Somewhere there must be a worldmaker.' The fact of the world drives us to God. As the astronomer Sir James Jeans has said, 'No astronomer can be an atheist.' The order of the world demands the mind of God behind it.

We might begin from *ourselves*. The one thing human beings have never created is life. We can alter and rearrange and change things; but we cannot create a living thing. Where then did we get our life? From our parents. Yes, but where did they get theirs? From their parents. But where did all this begin? At some time, life must have come into the world; and it must have come from outside the world, for human beings cannot create life; and once again we are driven back to God.

When we look in upon ourselves and out upon the world, we are driven to God. As the German philosopher Immanuel Kant said long ago, 'the moral law within us, and the starry heavens above us', drive us to God.

(2) Before we can show reverence for God, we must not only believe that God is, we must also know the kind of God he is. No one could show reverence for the Greek gods with their loves and wars, their hates and their adulteries, their trickeries and their mischief. No one can have reverence for capricious, immoral, impure gods. But, in God as we know him, there are three great qualities. There is *holiness*; there is *justice*; and there is *love*. We must show reverence for God not only because he exists, but because he is the God whom we know him to be.

(3) But people might believe that God is; they might be intellectually convinced that God is holy, just and loving; and still they might not have reverence. For reverence, there is necessary *a constant awareness of God*. To show reverence for God means to live in a God-filled world, to live a life in which we never forget God. This awareness is not confined to the Church or to so-called holy places; it must be an awareness which exists everywhere and at all times.

Wordsworth spoke of it in 'Lines composed above Tintern Abbey':

> *And I have felt*
> *A presence that disturbs me with the joy*

> *Of elevated thoughts; a sense sublime*
> *Of something far more deeply interfused,*
> *Whose dwelling is the light of setting suns,*
> *And the round ocean, and the living air,*
> *And the blue sky, and in the mind of man:*
> *A motion and a spirit, that impels*
> *All thinking things, all objects of all thought,*
> *And rolls through all things.*

One of the finest of modern devotional poets is Henry Ernest Hardy, who wrote under the name of Father Andrew. In 'The Mystic Beauty', he writes:

> *O London town has many moods,*
> *And mingled 'mongst its many broods*
> *A leavening of saints,*
>
> *And ever up and down its streets,*
> *If one has eyes to see one meets*
> *Stuff that an artist paints.*
>
> *I've seen a back street bathed in blue,*
> *Such as the soul of Whistler knew:*
> *A smudge of amber light,*
>
> *Where some fried fish-shop plied its trade,*
> *A perfect note of colour made –*
> *Oh, it was exquisite!*
>
> *I once came through St James' Park*
> *Betwixt the sunset and the dark,*
> *And oh the mystery*
>
> *Of grey and green and violet!*
> *I would I never might forget*
> *That evening harmony.*

I hold it true that God is there
If beauty breaks through anywhere;
And his most blessed feet,

Who once life's roughest roadway trod,
Who came as man to show us God,
Still pass along the street.

God in the back street, God in St James' Park, God in the fried fish shop – that is reverence. The trouble with most people is that their awareness of God is spasmodic, acute at certain times and places, totally absent at others. Reverence means the constant awareness of God.

(4) There remains one further ingredient in reverence. We must believe that God exists; we must know what kind of a God he is; we must be constantly aware of God. But people might have all these things and still not have reverence. To all these things must be added obedience and submission to God. Reverence is knowledge plus submission. In his catechism, Martin Luther asks: 'How is God's name hallowed among us?' and his answer is: 'When both our life and doctrine are truly Christian', that is to say, when our intellectual convictions, and our practical actions, are in full submission to the will of God.

To know that God is, to know what kind of a God he is, to be constantly aware of God, and to be constantly obedient to him – that is reverence, and that is what we pray for when we pray: 'Hallowed be your name.' Let God be given the reverence which his nature and character deserve.

God's kingdom and God's will

Matthew 6:10

Let your kingdom come:
Let your will be done, as in heaven, so also on earth.

THE phrase *the kingdom of God* is characteristic of the whole
New Testament. No phrase is used more often in prayer and
in preaching and in Christian literature. It is, therefore, of
primary importance that we should be clear as to what it
means.

It is evident that the kingdom of God was central to the
message of Jesus. The first emergence of Jesus on the scene
of history was when he came into Galilee preaching the
good news of the kingdom of God (Mark 1:14). Jesus himself
described the preaching of the kingdom as an obligation
laid upon him: 'I must proclaim the good news of the
kingdom of God to the other cities also; for I was sent for
this purpose' (Luke 4:43; Mark 1:38). Luke's description
of Jesus' activity is that he went through every city and
village preaching and showing the good news of the
kingdom of God (Luke 8:1). Clearly the meaning of the
kingdom of God is something which we are bound to try
to understand.

When we do try to understand the meaning of this
phrase, we meet with certain puzzling facts. We find that
Jesus spoke of the kingdom in three different ways. He
spoke of the kingdom as existing in the *past*. He said that
Abraham, Isaac and Jacob and all the prophets were in the
kingdom (Luke 13:28; Matthew 8:11). Clearly, therefore, the

kingdom goes far back into history. He spoke of the kingdom as *present*. 'The kingdom of God', he said, 'is among you' (Luke 17:21). The kingdom of God is therefore a present reality here and now. He spoke of the kingdom of God as *future*, for he taught the disciples to pray for the coming of the kingdom in this his own prayer. How then can the kingdom be past, present and future all at the one time? How can the kingdom be at one and the same time something which existed, which exists, and for whose coming it is our duty to pray?

We find the key in this double petition of the Lord's Prayer. One of the most common characteristics of Hebrew style is what is technically known as *parallelism*. The Hebrew language tends to say everything twice. A thing is said in one way, and then in another way which repeats or amplifies or explains the first way. Almost any verse of the Psalms will show this parallelism in action. Almost every verse of the Psalms divides in two in the middle, and the second half repeats or amplifies or explains the first half. Let us take some examples, and the point will become clear:

> *God is our refuge and strength,*
> *a very present help in trouble.*
>
> (Psalm 46:1)

> *The Lord of hosts is with us;*
> *the God of Jacob is our refuge.*
>
> (Psalm 46:7)

> *The Lord is my shepherd;*
>> *I shall not want.*
> *He makes me lie down in green pastures;*
>> *he leads me beside still waters.*

> (Psalm 23:1–2)

Let us apply this principle to these two petitions of the Lord's Prayer. Let us set them down side by side:

> *Your kingdom come,*
>> *Your will be done in earth as it is in heaven.*

Let us assume that the second petition explains and amplifies and defines the first. We then have the perfect definition of the kingdom of God – *The kingdom of God is a society upon earth where God's will is as perfectly done as it is in heaven*. Here we have the explanation of how the kingdom can be past, present and future all at the one time. Anyone who at any time in history perfectly did God's will was within the kingdom; anyone who perfectly does God's will is within the kingdom; but since the world is very far from being a place where God's will is perfectly and universally done, the consummation of the kingdom is still in the future and is still something for which we must pray.

To be in the kingdom is to obey the will of God. Immediately we see that the kingdom is not something which primarily has to do with nations and peoples and countries. It is something which has to do with each one of us. The kingdom is in fact the most personal thing in the world. The kingdom demands the submission of *my* will, *my* heart, *my* life. It is only when each one of us makes a personal decision and submission that the kingdom comes.

The Chinese Christian prayed the well-known prayer: 'Lord, revive your Church, beginning with me' – and we might well paraphrase that and say: 'Lord, bring in your kingdom, beginning with me.' To pray for the kingdom of heaven is to pray that *we* may submit our wills entirely to the will of God.

God's kingdom and God's will

Matthew 6:10 (*contd*)

FROM what we have already seen, it becomes clear that the most important thing in the world is to obey the will of God; the most important words in the world are 'Your will be done'. But it is equally clear that the frame of mind and the tone of voice in which these words are spoken will make a world of difference.

(1) Some people may say: 'Your will be done' in a tone of defeated resignation. They may say it not because they wish to say it, but because they have accepted the fact that they cannot possibly say anything else; they may say it because they have accepted the fact that God is too strong for them, and that it is useless to batter their heads against the walls of the universe. They may say it thinking only of the inescapable power of God which has them in its grip. As Edward Fitzgerald's *The Rubaiyat of Omar Khayyam* had it:

> But helpless Pieces of the Game He plays
> Upon this Chequer-board of Nights and Days;
>   Hither and thither moves, and checks, and slays,
> And one by one back in the closet lays.

> *The Ball no question makes of Ayes and Noes.*
> *But Here or There as strikes the Player goes;*
> *And He that Toss'd you down into the Field,*
> *He knows about it all – He knows – HE knows!*

Some people may accept the will of God for no other reason than that they have realized that they cannot do anything else.

(2) Some people may say: 'Your will be done' in a tone of bitter resentment. The poet Walter Swinburne spoke of feeling the trampling of the iron feet of God. In *Atalanta in Calydon*, he speaks of the supreme evil, God. Beethoven died all alone; and it is said that when they found his body his lips were drawn back in a snarl and his fists were clenched as if he were shaking his fists in the very face of God and of high heaven. Some may feel that God is their enemy, and yet an enemy so strong that they cannot resist. They may therefore accept God's will, but they may accept it with bitter resentment and smouldering anger.

(3) Some people may say: 'Your will be done' in perfect love and trust. They may say it gladly and willingly, no matter what that will may be. It should be easy for Christians to say: 'Your will be done' like that; for Christians can be very sure of two things about God.

(a) They can be sure of the *wisdom* of God. Sometimes when we want something built or constructed, or altered or repaired, we take it to the craftsman and consult him about it. He makes some suggestion, and we often end up by saying: 'Well, do what you think best. You are the expert.' God is the expert in life, and his guidance can never lead anyone astray.

When Richard Cameron, the Scottish Covenanter, was killed, his head and his hands were cut off by one Murray and taken to Edinburgh. 'His father being in prison for the same cause, the enemy carried them to him, to add grief unto his former sorrow, and inquired at him if he knew them. Taking his son's head and hands, which were very fair (being a man of fair complexion like himself), he kissed them and said, "I know them – I know them. They are my son's – my own dear son's. It is the Lord. Good is the will of the Lord, who cannot wrong me or mine, but hath made goodness and mercy to follow us all our days."' When a man can speak like that, when he is quite sure that his times are in the hands of the infinite wisdom of God, it is easy to say: 'Your will be done.'

(b) He can be sure of the *love* of God. We do not believe in a mocking and a capricious God, or in a blind and iron determinism. Thomas Hardy finishes his novel *Tess of the D'Urbervilles* with the grim words: 'The President of the Immortals had ended his sport with Tess.' We believe in a God whose name is love. As J. G. Whittier's hymn has it:

> *I know not where His islands lift*
> *Their fronded palms in air.*
> *I only know I cannot drift*
> *Beyond His love and care.*

As Robert Browning triumphantly declared his faith in lines from 'Paracelsus':

> *God, Thou art love! I build my faith on that ...*
> *I know thee who has kept my path and made*
> *Light for me in the darkness, tempering sorrow*

So that it reached me like a solemn joy.
It were too strange that I should doubt thy love.

And as Paul had it: 'He who did not withhold his own Son, but gave him up for all of us, will he not with him also give us everything else?' (Romans 8:32). No one can look at the cross and doubt the love of God; and when we are sure of the love of God, it is easy to say: 'Your will be done.'

Our daily bread

Matthew 6:11

Give us today bread for the coming day.

ONE would have thought that this is the one petition of the Lord's Prayer about the meaning of which there could have been no possible doubt. It seems on the face of it to be the simplest and the most direct of them all. But it is a fact that many interpreters have offered many interpretations of it. Before we think of its simple and obvious meaning, let us look at some of the other explanations which have been offered.

(1) The bread has been identified with the bread of the Lord's Supper. From the very beginning, the Lord's Prayer has been closely connected with the Lord's table. In the very first orders of service which we possess, it is always laid down that the Lord's Prayer should be prayed at the Lord's table, and some have taken this petition as a prayer to be granted the daily privilege of sitting at the table of our Lord, and of eating the spiritual food which men and women receive there.

(2) The bread has been identified with the spiritual food of the word of God. We sometimes sing the hymn:

> *Break thou the bread of life,*
> *Dear Lord, to me,*
> *As thou didst break the loaves*
> *Beside the sea.*
> *Beyond the sacred page*
> *I seek thee, Lord.*
> *My spirit pants for thee,*
> *O living word.*

So this petition has been taken to be a prayer for the true teaching, the true doctrine, the essential truth, which are in the Scriptures and the word of God, and which are indeed food for the mind and heart and soul.

(3) The bread has been taken to stand for Jesus himself. Jesus called himself *the bread of life* (John 6:33–5), and this has been taken to be a prayer that daily we may be fed on him who is the living bread. It was in that way that Matthew Arnold used the phrase, when he wrote his poem 'East London' about the saint of God he met in the East End of London one suffocating day:

> *'Twas August, and the fierce sun overhead*
> *Smote on the squalid streets of Bethnal Green,*
> *And the pale weaver, through his windows seen,*
> *In Spitalfields, look'd thrice dispirited.*
>
> *I met a preacher there I knew and said:*
> *'Ill and o'er worked, how fare you in this scene?'*
> *'Bravely!' said he, 'for I of late have been*

Much cheer'd with thoughts of Christ, the living
    bread.'

So, this petition has been taken as a prayer that we too might be cheered and strengthened with Christ the living bread.

(4) This petition has been taken in a purely Jewish sense. The bread has been taken to be the bread of the heavenly kingdom. Luke tells how one of the bystanders said to Jesus: 'Blessed is anyone who will eat bread in the kingdom of God' (Luke 14:15). The Jews had a strange yet vivid idea. They held that when the Messiah came, and when the golden age dawned, there would be what they called the messianic banquet, at which the chosen ones of God would sit down. The slain bodies of the monsters Behemoth and Leviathan would provide the meat and the fish courses of the banquet. It would be a kind of reception feast given by God to his own people. So, this has been taken to be a petition for a place at the final messianic banquet of the people of God.

Although we need not agree that any one of these explanations is the main meaning of this petition, we need not reject any of them as false. They all have their own truth and their own relevance.

The difficulty of interpreting this petition was increased by the fact that there was very considerable doubt as to the meaning of the word *epiousios*, which is the word translated in the Revised Standard Version as *daily*. The extraordinary fact was that, until a short time ago, there was no other known occurrence of this word in the whole of Greek literature. The third-century Christian scholar Origen knew this, and indeed held that Matthew had invented the word.

It was therefore not possible to be sure what it precisely meant. But not very long ago a papyrus fragment turned up with this word on it; and the papyrus fragment was actually a woman's shopping list! And against an item on it was the word *epiousios*. It was a note to remind her to buy supplies of a certain food for the coming day. So, very simply, what this petition means is: 'Give me the things we need to eat for this coming day. Help me to get the things I've got on my shopping list when I go out this morning. Give me the things we need to eat when the children come in from school, and the family come in from work. Grant that the table is not bare when we sit down together today.' This is a simple prayer that God will supply us with the things we need for the coming day.

Our daily bread

Matthew 6:11 (*contd*)

WHEN we see that this is a simple petition for our everyday needs, certain tremendous truths emerge from it.

(1) It tells us that God cares for our bodies. Jesus showed us that; he spent so much time healing people's diseases and satisfying physical hunger. He was anxious when he thought that the crowd who had followed him out into the lonely places had a long journey home, and no food to eat before they set out upon it. We do well to remember that God is interested in our bodies. Any teaching which belittles, despises and slanders the body is wrong. We can see what God thinks of our human bodies, when we remember that he himself in

Jesus Christ took a human body upon him. It is not simply *soul* salvation, it is *whole* salvation, the salvation of body, mind and spirit, at which Christianity aims.

(2) This petition teaches us to pray for our *daily* bread, for bread *for the coming day*. It teaches us to live one day at a time, and not to worry and be anxious about the distant and the unknown future. When Jesus taught his disciples to pray this petition, there is little doubt that his mind was going back to the story of the manna in the wilderness (Exodus 16:1–21). The children of Israel were starving in the wilderness, and God sent them the manna, the food from heaven; but there was one condition – they must gather only enough for their immediate needs. If they tried to gather too much, and to store it up, it went bad. They had to be satisfied with enough for the day. As one Rabbi put it: 'The portion of a day in its day, because he who created the day created sustenance for the day.' And as another Rabbi had it: 'He who possesses what he can eat today, and says, "What shall I eat tomorrow?" is a man of little faith.' This petition tells us to live one day at a time. It forbids the anxious worry which is so characteristic of the life which has not learned to trust God.

(3) By implication, this petition gives God his proper place. It admits that it is from God we receive the food which is necessary to support life. No one has ever created a seed which will grow. The scientist can analyse a seed into its constituent elements, but no synthetic seed would ever grow. All living things come from God. Our food, therefore, is the direct gift of God.

(4) This petition very wisely reminds us of how prayer works. If people prayed this prayer, and then sat back and waited for bread to fall into their hands, they would certainly

starve. It reminds us that prayer and work go hand in hand and that when we pray we must go on to work to make our prayers come true. It is true that the living seed comes from God, but it is equally true that it is our task to grow and to cultivate that seed. Dick Sheppard, the famous pacifist and preacher, used to love a certain story. There was a man who had an allotment; he had with great toil reclaimed a piece of ground, clearing away the stones, eradicating the rank growth of weeds, enriching and feeding the ground, until it produced the loveliest flowers and vegetables. One evening he was showing a pious friend around his allotment. The pious friend said: 'It's wonderful what God can do with a bit of ground like this, isn't it?' 'Yes,' said the man who had put in such toil, 'but you should have seen this bit of ground when God had it to himself!' God's bounty and human toil must combine. Prayer, like faith, without works is dead. When we pray this petition, we are recognizing two basic truths – that without God we can do nothing, and that without our effort and co-operation God can do nothing for us.

(5) We must note that Jesus did not teach us to pray: 'Give *me my* daily bread.' He taught us to pray: 'Give *us our* daily bread.' The problem of the world is not that there is not enough to go round; there is enough and to spare. The problem is not the *supply* of life's essentials; it is the *distribution* of them. This prayer teaches us never to be selfish in our prayers. It is a prayer which we can help God to answer by giving to others who are less fortunate than we are. This prayer is not only a prayer that we may *receive* our daily bread; it is also a prayer that we may *share* our daily bread with others.

Forgiveness human and divine

Matthew 6:12, 14–15

> *Forgive us our debts as we forgive our debtors … For, if*
> *you forgive men their trespasses, your heavenly Father will*
> *forgive you too; but if you do not forgive men their trespasses,*
> *neither will your Father forgive your trespasses.*

BEFORE we can honestly pray this petition of the Lord's Prayer, we must realize that we need to pray it. That is to say, before we can pray this petition we must have a sense of sin. Sin is not nowadays a popular word. Men and women rather resent being called, or treated as, hell-deserving sinners.

The trouble is that most people have a wrong conception of sin. They would readily agree that the burglar, the drunkard, the murderer, the adulterer and the foul-mouthed person are sinners. But they themselves are guilty of none of these sins; they live decent, ordinary, respectable lives, and have never even been in danger of appearing in court, or going to prison, or achieving some notoriety in the newspapers. They therefore feel that sin has nothing to do with them.

The New Testament uses five different words for *sin*.

(1) The most common word is *hamartia*. This was originally a shooting word and means *a missing of the target*. To fail to hit the target was *hamartia*. Therefore *sin is the failure to be what we might have been and could have been.*

The nineteenth-century writer Charles Lamb has a picture of a man named Samuel le Grice. Le Grice was a brilliant youth who never fulfilled his promise. Lamb says that there were three stages in his career. There was a time when people said: 'He will do something.' There was a time when people said: 'He could do something if he would.' There was a time when people said: 'He might have done something, if he had liked.' The poet Edwin Muir writes in his *Autobiography*: 'After a certain age all of us, good and bad, are grief-stricken because of powers within us which have never been realized: because, in other words, we are not what we should be.'

That precisely is *hamartia*; and that is precisely the situation in which we are all involved. Are we as good husbands or wives as we could be? Are we as good sons or daughters as we could be? Are we as good workers or employers as we could be? Can any one of us dare to claim that we are all we might have been, and have done all we could have done? When we realize that sin means the failure to hit the target, the failure to be all that we might have been and could have been, then it is clear that every one of us is a sinner.

(2) The second word for sin is *parabasis*, which literally means *a stepping across. Sin is the stepping across the line which is drawn between right and wrong.*

Do we always stay on the right side of the line which divides honesty and dishonesty? Is there never any such thing as a petty dishonesty in our lives?

Do we always stay on the right side of the line which divides truth and falsehood? Do we never, by word or by silence, twist or evade or distort the truth?

Do we always stay on the right side of the line which divides kindness and courtesy from selfishness and harshness? Is there never an unkind action or a discourteous word in our lives?

When we think of it in this way, there can be none who can claim always to have remained on the right side of the dividing line.

(3) The third word for sin is *paraptōma*, which means *a slipping across*. It is the kind of slip which someone might make on a slippery or an icy road. It is not so deliberate as *parabasis*. Again and again, we speak of words 'slipping out'; again and again, we are swept away by some impulse or passion which has momentarily gained control of us and which has made us lose our self-control. The best of us can slip into sin when for the moment we are off our guard.

(4) The fourth word for sin is *anomia*, which means *lawlessness*. *Anomia* is the sin of the person who knows the right, and who yet does the wrong; the sin of the one who knows the law, and who yet breaks the law. The first of all the human instincts is the instinct to do what we like; and therefore there come into many people's lives times when they wish to kick over the traces and to defy the law, and to do or to take the forbidden thing. In 'Mandalay', Rudyard Kipling makes the old soldier say:

> *Ship me somewheres east of Suez, where the best is like the worst,*
> *Where there aren't no Ten Commandments, an' a man can raise a thirst.*

Even if there are some who can say that they have never broken any of the Ten Commandments, there are none who can say that they have never wished to break any of them.

(5) The fifth word for sin is the word *opheilēma*, which is the word used in the body of the Lord's Prayer;

and *opheilēma* means *a debt*. It means *a failure to pay that which is due*, a failure in duty. None of us could ever dare to claim that we have perfectly fulfilled our duty to other people and to God: such perfection does not exist in this world.

So, when we come to see what sin really is, we come to see that it is a universal disease in which we are all involved. Outward respectability in the sight of others and inward sinfulness in the sight of God may well go hand in hand. This, in fact, is a petition of the Lord's Prayer which we all need to pray.

Forgiveness human and divine

Matthew 6:12, 14–15 (*contd*)

NOT only do we need to realize that we need to pray this petition of the Lord's Prayer; we also need to realize what we are doing when we pray it. Of all the petitions of the Lord's Prayer, this is the most frightening.

'Forgive us our debts as we forgive our debtors.' The literal meaning is: 'Forgive us our sins *in proportion as* we forgive those who have sinned against us.' In verses 14 and 15, Jesus says in the plainest possible language that if we forgive others, God will forgive us; but if we refuse to forgive others, God will refuse to forgive us. It is, therefore, quite clear that if we pray this petition with an unhealed breach, an unsettled quarrel in our lives, we are asking God *not* to forgive us.

If we say: 'I will never forgive so-and-so for what he or she has done to me,' if we say: 'I will never forget what so-

and-so did to me,' and then go and take this petition on our lips, we are quite deliberately asking God not to forgive us. As someone has put it: 'Forgiveness, like peace, is one and indivisible.' Human forgiveness and divine forgiveness are inextricably intertwined. Our forgiveness of one another and God's forgiveness of us cannot be separated; they are interlinked and interdependent. If we remembered what we are doing when we take this petition on our lips, there would be times when we would not dare to pray it.

When Robert Louis Stevenson lived in the South Sea Islands, he always used to conduct family worship in the mornings for his household. It always concluded with the Lord's Prayer. One morning, in the middle of the Lord's Prayer, he rose from his knees and left the room. His health was always precarious, and his wife followed him thinking that he was ill. 'Is there anything wrong?' she said. 'Only this,' said Stevenson. 'I am not fit to pray the Lord's Prayer today.' None of us is fit to pray the Lord's Prayer so long as the unforgiving spirit holds sway within our hearts. If we have not put things right with our neighbours, we cannot put things right with God.

If we are to have this Christian forgiveness in our lives, three things are necessary.

(1) We must learn *to understand*. There is always a reason why people do things. If they are boorish and impolite and bad-tempered, maybe they are worried or in pain. If they treat us with suspicion and dislike, maybe they have misunderstood, or have been misinformed about something we have said or done. Maybe they are victims of their own environment or their own heredity. Maybe they find life difficult, and human relations are a problem for them. Forgiveness would be very

much easier for us if we tried to understand before we allowed ourselves to condemn.

(2) We must learn *to forget*. As long as we brood upon a snub or an insult, there is no hope that we will forgive. We so often say: 'I can't forget what so-and-so did to me,' or: 'I will never forget how I was treated by such-and-such a person or in such-and-such a place.' These are dangerous sayings, because we can in the end make it humanly impossible for us to forget. We can print the memory indelibly upon our minds.

The famous Scottish man of letters, Andrew Lang, once wrote and published a very kind review of a book by a young man. The young man repaid him with a bitter and insulting attack. About three years later, Andrew Lang was staying with Robert Bridges, the Poet Laureate. Bridges saw Lang reading a certain book. 'Why,' he said, 'that's another book by that ungrateful young cub who behaved so shamefully to you.' To his astonishment, he found that Andrew Lang's mind was a blank on the whole affair. He had completely forgotten the bitter and insulting attack. To forgive, said Bridges, was the sign of greatness, but to forget was sublime. Nothing but the cleansing spirit of Christ can take from these memories of ours the old bitterness that we must forget.

(3) We must learn *to love*. We have already seen that Christian love, *agapē,* is that unconquerable benevolence, that undefeatable goodwill, which will never seek anything but the highest good of others, no matter what they do to us, and no matter how they treat us. That love can come to us only when Christ, who is that love, comes to dwell within our hearts – and he cannot come unless we invite him.

To be forgiven we must forgive, and that is a condition of forgiveness which only the power of Christ can enable us to fulfil.

The ordeal of temptation

Matthew 6:13

> *And lead us not into temptation, but deliver us from the evil one.*

THERE are two matters of meaning at which we must look before we begin to study this petition in detail.

(1) To modern ears, the word *tempt* is always a bad word; it always means *to seek to seduce into evil*. But in the Bible the verb *peirazein* is often better translated by the word *test* than by the word *tempt*. In its New Testament usage, to *tempt* people is not so much to seek to seduce them into sin as it is to test their strength and their loyalty and their ability for service.

In the Old Testament, we read the story of how God tested the loyalty of Abraham by seeming to demand the sacrifice of his only son Isaac. In the Authorized Version, the story begins: 'And it came to pass that God did *tempt* Abraham' (Genesis 22:1). Obviously the word *tempt* cannot there mean to seek to seduce into sin, for that is something that God would never do. It means rather to submit to a test of loyalty and obedience. When we read the story of the temptations of Jesus, it begins: 'Then Jesus was led up by the Spirit into the wilderness to be *tempted* by the devil' (Matthew 4:1). If we take the word *tempt* there in the sense of to seduce into sin, it makes the Holy Spirit a partner in an attempt to compel Jesus to sin. Time and again in the Bible, we will find that the word *tempt* has the idea of *testing* in it, at least as much as the idea of seeking to lead into sin.

Here, then, is one of the great and precious truths about temptation. Temptation is not designed to make us fall. Temptation is designed to make us stronger and better men and women. Temptation is not designed to make us sinners. It is designed to make us good. We may fail in the test, but we are not meant to. We are meant to emerge stronger and finer. In one sense, temptation is not so much the *penalty* of being human; it is the glory of being human. If metal is to be used in a great engineering project, it is tested at stresses and strains far beyond those which it is ever likely to have to bear. So we have to be tested before God can use us greatly in his service.

All that is true; but it is also true that the Bible is never in any doubt that there is a power of evil in this world. The Bible is not a speculative book, and it does not discuss the origin of that power of evil, but it knows that it is there. Quite certainly, this petition of the Lord's Prayer should be translated not as 'Deliver us from evil' but as 'Deliver us from the evil one.' The Bible thinks of evil not as an abstract principle or force, but as an active, personal power in opposition to God.

The development of the idea of Satan in the Bible is of the greatest interest. In Hebrew, the word *Satan* simply means an *adversary*. It can often be used of human beings. A person's adversary is called *Satan*. In the Authorized Version, the Philistines are afraid that David may turn out to be their *Satan* (1 Samuel 29:4); Solomon declares that God has given him such peace and prosperity that there is no *Satan* left to oppose him (1 Kings 5:4); David regards Abishai as his *Satan* (2 Samuel 19:22). In all these cases, *Satan* means an *adversary* or *opponent*. From that, the word *Satan* goes on to mean *one who pleads a case against someone*. Then the word leaves earth and, as it were, enters heaven. The Jews had the idea that in heaven there was an angel whose charge it was to state the case against an individual, a kind of prosecuting angel; and that became the function of *Satan*. At that stage, Satan is not an evil power: he is part of the judgment apparatus of heaven. In Job 1:6, Satan is numbered among the sons of God: 'One day the heavenly beings came to present themselves before the Lord, and Satan also came among them.' At this stage, Satan is the divine prosecutor of human beings.

But it is not so very great a step from *stating* a case against an individual to *making up a case* against that person. And that is the next step. The other name of Satan is the devil; and *devil* comes from the Greek word *diabolos*, which is the regular word for a *slanderer*. So *Satan* becomes the *devil*, the slanderer *par excellence*, the adversary of men and women, the power who is out to frustrate the purposes of God and to ruin the human race. Satan comes to stand for everything which is anti-human and anti-God. It is from that ruining power that Jesus teaches us to pray to be delivered. The origin of that power is not discussed; there are no speculations. As someone has put it – if we wake up and find the house on fire, we do not sit down in a chair and write or read a treatise on the origin of fires in private houses; we set out to try to extinguish the fire and to save the house. So the Bible wastes no time in speculations about the origin of evil. It equips people to fight the battle against the evil which is unquestionably there.

The attack of temptation

Matthew 6:13 (*contd*)

LIFE is always under attack from temptation, but no enemy can launch an invasion until a bridgehead has been found. Where then does temptation find its bridgehead? Where do our temptations come from? To be forewarned is to be forearmed, and if we know where the attack is likely to come from, we will have a better chance to overcome it.

(1) Sometimes the attack of temptation comes from outside us. There are people whose influence is bad. There are people in whose company it would be very difficult even to suggest doing a dishonourable thing, and there are people in whose company it is easy to do the wrong things. When Robert Burns was a young man, he went to Irvine to learn flax-dressing. There he fell in with a certain Robert Brown, who was a man who had seen much of the world, and who had a fascinating and a dominating personality. Burns tells us that he admired him and strove to imitate him. Burns goes on: 'He was the only man I ever saw who was a greater fool than myself when Woman was the guiding star ... He spoke of a certain fashionable failing with levity, which hitherto I had regarded with horror ... Here his friendship did me a mischief.' There are friendships and associations which can do us a mischief. In a tempting world, we should be very careful in our choice of friends and of the society in which we will move. We should give the temptations which come from outside as little chance as possible.

(2) It is one of the tragic facts of life that temptations can come to us from those who love us; and of all kinds of

temptation, this is the hardest to fight. It comes from people who love us and who have not the slightest intention of harming us.

The kind of thing that happens is this. We may know that we ought to take a certain course of action; we may feel divinely drawn to a certain career; but to follow that course of action may involve unpopularity and risk; to accept that career may be to give up all that the world calls success. It may well be that in such circumstances those who love us will seek to dissuade us from acting as we know we ought, and they will do so because they love us. They counsel caution, prudence, worldly wisdom; they want to see those they love do well in a worldly sense; they do not wish to see us throw our chances away; and so they seek to stop us doing what we know to be right for us.

In 'Gareth and Lynette', Tennyson tells the story of Gareth, the youngest son of Lot and Bellicent. Gareth wishes to join his brothers in the service of King Arthur. Bellicent, his mother, does not wish him to go. 'Hast thou no pity on my loneliness?' she asks. His father Lot is old and lies 'like a log all but smouldered out'. Both his brothers have gone to Arthur's court. Must he go too? If he will stay at home, she will arrange the hunt, and find him a princess for his bride, and make him happy. It was because she loved him that she wished to keep him; the tempter was speaking with the very voice of love. But Gareth answers:

> *O mother,*
> *How can you keep me tethered to you – shame.*
> *Man am I grown, and man's work must I do.*

Follow the deer? Follow Christ the King.
Live pure, speak true, right wrong, follow the King –
Else, wherefore born?

The youth went out, but the voice of love tempted him to stay.

That was what happened to Jesus. 'One's foes', said Jesus, 'will be members of one's own household' (Matthew 10:36). They came and tried to take him home, because they said that he was mad (Mark 3:21). To them he seemed to be throwing his life and his career away; to them he seemed to be making a fool of himself; and they tried to stop him. Sometimes the bitterest of all temptations come to us from the voice of love.

(3) There is one very odd way in which temptation can come, especially to younger people. There is in most of us a peculiar streak which, at least in certain company, makes us wish to appear worse than we are. We do not wish to appear soft and pious, namby-pamby and holy. We would rather be thought daredevil, bold adventurers, men and women of the world and not innocents. St Augustine has a famous passage in his confessions: 'Among my equals I was ashamed of being less shameless than others, when I heard them boast of their wickedness ... And I took pleasure not only in the pleasure of the deed but in the praise ... I made myself worse than I was, that I might not be reproached, and when in anything I had not sinned as the most abandoned ones, I would say that I had done what I had not done, that I might not seem contemptible.' Many people have begun on some addiction, or introduced themselves to some habit, because they did not wish to appear less experienced in worldliness than

the company in which they happened to be. One of the great defences against temptation is simply the courage to be good.

The attack of temptation

Matthew 6:13 (*contd*)

(4) BUT temptation comes not only from outside us; it comes from inside us too. If there was nothing in us to which temptation could appeal, then it would be helpless to defeat us. In every one of us, there is some weak spot; and at that weak spot, temptation launches its attack.

The point of vulnerability differs in all of us. What is a violent temptation to one person leaves another quite unmoved; and what leaves one person quite unmoved may be an irresistible temptation to another. J. M. Barrie wrote a play called *The Will*. Mr Devizes, the lawyer, noticed that an old clerk, who had been in his service for many years, was looking very ill. He asked him if anything was the matter. The old man told him that his doctor had informed him that he was suffering from an incurable and ultimately fatal disease.

> Mr DEVIZES [*uncomfortably*]: *I'm sure it's not – what you fear. Any specialist would tell you so.*
> SURTEES [*without looking up*]: *I've been to one, sir – yesterday.*
> Mr DEVIZES: *Well?*
> SURTEES: *It's – that, sir.*
> Mr DEVIZES: *He couldn't be sure.*

Surtees: Yes, sir.

Mr *Devizes:* An operation –

Surtees: Too late for that, he said. If I had been operated on long ago, I might have had a chance.

Mr *Devizes:* But you didn't have it long ago.

Surtees: Not to my knowledge, sir; but he says it was there all the same, always in me, a black spot, not as big as a pin's head, but waiting to spread and destroy me in the fullness of time.

Mr *Devizes* [helpless]: It seems damnably unfair.

Surtees [humbly]: I don't know, sir. He says there is a spot of that kind in pretty nigh all of us, and, if we don't look out, it does for us in the end.

Mr *Devizes:* No. No. No.

Surtees: He called it the accursed thing. I think he meant we should know of it, and be on the watch.

In each one of us there is the weak spot, which, if we are not on the watch, can ruin us. Somewhere within us there is the flaw, some fault of temperament which can ruin life, some instinct or passion so strong that it may at any time snap the leash, some quirk in our make-up that makes what is a pleasure to someone else a menace to us. We should realize it, and be on the watch.

(5) But, strangely enough, temptation comes sometimes not from our weakest point, but from our strongest point. If there is one thing of which we are in the habit of saying: 'That is one thing anyway which I would never do,' it is just there that we should be upon the watch. History is full of the stories of fortresses which were taken just at the point where the defenders thought them so strong that no guard

was necessary. Nothing gives temptation its chance like over-confidence. At our weakest and at our strongest points, we must be on our guard.

The defence against temptation

Matthew 6:13 (*contd*)

We have thought of the attack of temptation; let us now assemble our defences against temptation.

(1) There is the simple defence of *self-respect*. When Nehemiah's life was in danger, it was suggested that he should quit his work and shut himself in the Temple until the danger was past. His answer was: 'Should a man like me run away? Would a man like me go into the temple to save his life? I will not go in!' (Nehemiah 6:11). People may escape many things, but they cannot escape themselves. They must live with their memories; and if they have lost their self-respect, life becomes intolerable. Once the American President James Garfield was urged to take a profitable, but dishonourable, course of action. It was said: 'No one will ever know.' His answer was: 'President Garfield will know – and I've got to sleep with him.' When we are tempted, we may well defend ourselves by saying: 'Is someone like me going to do a thing like that?'

(2) There is the defence of *tradition*. None of us can lightly fail the traditions and the heritage into which we have entered, and which have taken generations to build up. When Pericles, the greatest of the statesmen of Athens, was going to address the Athenian Assembly, he always whispered to himself:

'Pericles, remember that you are an Athenian and that you go to speak to Athenians.'

One of the epics of the Second World War was the defence of Tobruk. The Coldstream Guards cut their way out of Tobruk, but only a handful of them survived, and even these were just shadows of men. The Royal Air Force (RAF) was caring for 200 survivors out of two battalions. A Coldstream Guards officer was in the mess. Another officer said to him: 'After all, as Foot Guards, you had no option but to have a go.' And an RAF man standing there said: 'It must be pretty tough to be in the Brigade of Guards, because tradition compels you to carry on irrespective of circumstances.'

The power of a tradition is one of the greatest things in life. We belong to a country, a school, a family, a church. What we do affects that to which we belong. We cannot lightly betray the traditions into which we have entered.

(3) There is the defence of *those whom we love and those who love us*. Many people would sin if the only penalty they had to bear was the penalty they would have to bear themselves; but they are saved from sin because they could not meet the pain that would appear in someone's eyes, if they made shipwreck of their lives.

The American novelist Laura E. Richards has a parable like this:

> *A man sat by the door of his house smoking his pipe, and his neighbour sat beside him and tempted him. 'You are poor,' said the neighbour, 'and you are out of work and here is a way of bettering yourself. It will be an easy job and it will bring in money, and it is no more dishonest than things that are done every day by respectable people. You will be*

> *a fool to throw away such a chance as this. Come with me*
> *and we will settle the matter at once.' And the man listened.*
> *Just then his young wife came to the door of the cottage*
> *and she had her baby in her arms. 'Will you hold the baby*
> *for a minute,' she said. 'He is fretful and I must hang out*
> *the clothes to dry.' The man took the baby and held him on*
> *his knees. And as he held him, the child looked up, and*
> *the eyes of the child spoke: 'I am flesh of your flesh,' said*
> *the child's eyes. 'I am soul of your soul. Where you lead I*
> *shall follow. Lead the way, father. My feet come after yours.'*
> *Then said the man to his neighbour: 'Go, and come here no*
> *more.'*

Some people might be perfectly willing to pay the price of sin if that price affected only themselves. But if they remember that their sin will break someone else's heart, they will have a strong defence against temptation.

(4) There is the defence of *the presence of Jesus Christ*. Jesus is not a figure in a book; he is a living presence. Sometimes we ask: 'What would you do, if you suddenly found Christ standing beside you? How would you live, if Jesus Christ was a guest in your house?' But the whole point of the Christian faith is that Jesus Christ *is* beside us, and he *is* a guest in every home. His is the inescapable presence, and, therefore, we must make all life fit for him to see. We have a strong defence against temptation in the memory of the continual presence of Jesus Christ.

The Gospel of Luke – setting the context

A historian's care

First and foremost, Luke's gospel is an exceedingly careful bit of work. His Greek is notably good. The first four verses are well-nigh the best Greek in the New Testament. In them he claims that his work is the product of the most careful research. His opportunities were ample and his sources must have been good. As the trusted companion of Paul he must have known all the great figures of the Church, and we may be sure that he had them tell their stories to him. For two years he was Paul's companion in imprisonment in Caesarea. In those long days he had every opportunity for study and research and he must have used them well.

An example of Luke's care is the way in which he dates the emergence of John the Baptist. He does so by no fewer than six contemporary datings. 'In the fifteenth year of the reign of Tiberius Caesar [1], Pontius Pilate being governor of Judaea [2], Herod being tetrarch of Galilee [3], and his brother Philip being tetrarch of the region of Ituraea and Trachonitis [4], and Lysanias tetrarch of Abilene [5] in the high priesthood of Annas and Caiaphas [6], the word of God came to John' (Luke 3:1–2, Revised Standard Version). Here is a man who is writing with care and who will be as accurate as it is possible for him to be.

The gospel for the Gentiles

It is clear that Luke wrote mainly for Gentiles. The book was written tgo a man called Theophilus, a high official in the Roman government. Theophilus was a Gentile, as was Luke himself, and there is nothing in the gospel that a Gentile could not grasp and understand. (1) As we have seen, Luke begins his dating from the reigning *Roman* emperor and the current *Roman* governor. The *Roman* date comes first. (2) Unlike Matthew, he is not greatly interested in the life of Jesus as the fulfilment of Jewish prophecy. (3) He very seldom quotes the Old Testament at all. (4) He has a habit of giving Hebrew words in their Greek equivalent so that a Greek would understand. Simon the *Cananaean* becomes Simon the *Zealot* (cf. Luke 6:15; Matthew 10:4). *Calvary* is called not by its Hebrew name, *Golgotha*, but by its Greek name, *Kranion*. Both mean *the place of a skull*. He never uses the Jewish term *Rabbi* of Jesus but always a Greek word meaning *Master*. When he is tracing the descent of Jesus, he traces it not to Abraham, the founder of the Jewish race, as Matthew does, but to Adam, the founder of the human race (cf. Matthew 1:2; Luke 3:38). Because of this Luke is the easiest of all the gospels to read.

The gospel of praise

In Luke the phrase *praising God* occurs oftener than in all the rest of the New Testament put together. This praise reaches its peak in the three great hymns that the Church has sung throughout all her generations – the *Magnificat* (1:46–55), the *Benedictus* (1:68–79) and the *Nunc Dimittis* (2:29–32). There is a radiance in Luke's gospel which is a lovely thing, as if the sheen of heaven had touched the things of earth.

The Universal Gospel

But the outstanding characteristic of Luke is that it is the universal gospel. All the barriers are down; Jesus Christ is for all people without distinction.

(a) The kingdom of heaven is not shut to the Samaritans (9:51–6). Luke alone tells the parable of the Good Samaritan (10:30–7). The one grateful leper is a Samaritan (17:11–19). John can record a saying that the Jews have no dealings with the Samaritans (John 4:9). But Luke refuses to shut the door on anyone.

(b) Luke shows Jesus speaking with approval of Gentiles whom an orthodox Jew would have considered unclean. He shows us Jesus citing the widow of Zarephath and Naaman the Syrian as shining examples (4:25–7). The Roman centurion is praised for the greatness of his faith (7:9). Luke tells us of that great word of Jesus, 'People will come from east and west, from north and south, and will eat in the kingdom of God' (13:29).

(c) Luke is supremely interested in the poor. When Mary brings the offering for her purification it is the offering of the poor (2:24). When Jesus is, as it were, setting out his credentials to the emissaries of John, the climax is, 'The poor have good news brought to them' (7:22). He alone tells the parable of the rich man and the poor man (16:19–31).

In Luke's account of the beatitudes the saying of Jesus runs, not, as in Matthew (5:3), 'Blessed are the poor in spirit', but simply, 'Blessed are you who are poor' (Luke 6:20). Luke's gospel has been called 'the gospel of the underdog'. His heart runs out to everyone for whom life is an unequal struggle.

(d) Above all Luke shows Jesus as the friend of outcasts and sinners. He alone tells of the woman who anointed Jesus' feet and bathed them with her tears and wiped them with her hair in the house of Simon the Pharisee (7:36–50); of Zachaeus, the despised tax-gatherer (19:1–10); of the penitent thief (23:43); and he alone has the immortal story of the prodigal son and the loving father (15:11–32). When Matthew tells how Jesus sent his disciples out to preach, he says that Jesus told them not to go to the Samaritans or the Gentiles (Matthew 10:5); but Luke omits that altogether. All four gospel writers quote from Isaiah 40 when they give the message of John the Baptist, 'Prepare the way of the Lord; make straight in the desert a highway for our God'; but only Luke continues the quotation to its triumphant conclusion, 'And all flesh shall see the salvation of God' (Isaiah 40:3–5; Matthew 3:3; Mark 1:3; John 1:23; Luke 3:4, 6). Luke of all the gospel writers sees no limits to the love of God.

The Lord's Prayer according to the Gospel of Luke

Teach us to pray

Luke 11:1–4

> Jesus was praying in a certain place, and when he stopped,
> one of his disciples said to him, 'Lord, teach us to pray, as
> John taught his disciples.' He said to them, 'When you pray,
> say,
>
>> O Father, let your name be held in reverence.
>> Let your kingdom come.
>> Give to us each day our bread for the day.
>> And forgive us our sins as we too forgive
>>   everyone who is in debt to us.
>> And lead us not into temptation.'

It was the regular custom for a Rabbi to teach his disciples
a simple prayer which they might habitually use. John had
done that for his disciples, and now Jesus' disciples came
asking him to do the same for them. This is Luke's version
of the Lord's Prayer. It is shorter than Matthew's, but it will
teach us all we need to know about how to pray and what
to pray for.

(1) It begins by calling God *Father*. That was the characteristic
Christian address to God (cf. Galatians 4:6; Romans 8:15;

1 Peter 1:17). The very first word tells us that in prayer we are not coming to someone out of whom gifts have to be unwillingly extracted, but to a father who delights to supply his children's needs.

(2) In Hebrew *the name* means much more than merely the name by which a person is called. *The name* means the whole character of the person as it is revealed and known to us. Psalm 9:10 says, 'Those who know your name put their trust in you.' That means far more than knowing that God's name is Yahweh. It means that those who know the whole character and mind and heart of God will gladly put their trust in him.

(3) We must note particularly the order of the Lord's Prayer. Before anything is asked for ourselves, God and his glory, and the reverence due to him, come first. Only when we give God his place will other things take their proper place.

(4) The prayer covers all life.

(a) It covers *present need*. It tells us to pray for our daily bread; but it is bread *for the day* for which we pray. This goes back to the old story of the manna in the wilderness (Exodus 16:11–21). Only enough for the needs of the day might be gathered. We are not to worry about the unknown future, but to live a day at a time. As Cardinal Newman wrote in that well-loved hymn 'Lead Kindly Light':

> *I do not ask to see*
> *The distant scene – one step enough for me.*

(b) It covers *past sin*. When we pray we cannot do other than pray for forgiveness, for even the best of us is a sinner coming before the purity of God.

(c) It covers *future trials*. *Temptation* means any testing situation. It includes far more than the mere seduction to sin; it covers every situation which is a challenge to and a test of a person's humanity and integrity and fidelity. We cannot escape it, but we can meet it with God.

Someone has said that the Lord's Prayer has two great uses in our private prayers. If we use it at the beginning of our devotions it awakens all kinds of holy desires which lead us on into the right pathways of prayer. If we use it at the end of our devotions it sums up all we ought to pray for in the presence of God.